"Emotional and sensory regulation can present as an insurmountable obstacle when difficulties arise and affects behaviors and everyday tasks. Brukner not only tackles these issues head on, but does it from a perspective of an expert occupational therapist and mother. This allows for sensible practicality teamed with proven evidence-based research that truly garners results."

—*Dr. Frederick B. Covington, OTD*
www.ontimepediatrics.com

by the same author

How to Be a Superhero Called Self-Control!
Super Powers to Help Younger Children
to Regulate their Emotions and Senses
Lauren Brukner
Illustrated by Apsley
ISBN 978 1 84905 717 2
eISBN 978 1 78450 203 4

The Kids' Guide to Staying Awesome and In Control
Simple Stuff to Help Children Regulate their Emotions and Senses
Lauren Brukner
Illustrated by Apsley
ISBN 978 1 84905 997 8
eISBN 978 0 85700 962 3

of related interest

Seahorse's Magical Sun Sequences
How All Children (and Sea Creatures) Can Use Yoga to Feel
Positive, Confident and Completely Included
Michael Chissick
Illustrated by Sarah Peacock
ISBN 978 1 84819 283 6
eISBN 978 0 85701 230 2

Sitting on a Chicken
The Best (Ever) 52 Yoga Games to Teach in Schools
Michael Chissick
Illustrated by Sarah Peacock
ISBN 978 1 84819 325 3
eISBN 978 0 85701 280 7

Starving the Anxiety Gremlin
A Cognitive Behavioural Therapy Workbook on
Anxiety Management for Young People
Kate Collins-Donnelly
ISBN 978 1 84905 341 9
eISBN 978 0 85700 673 8

Starving the Anger Gremlin
A Cognitive Behavioural Therapy Workbook
on Anger Management for Young People
Kate Collins-Donnelly
ISBN 978 1 84905 286 3
eISBN 978 0 85700 621 9

STAY COOL AND IN CONTROL WITH THE
KEEP-CALM GURU

Wise Ways for Children to Regulate their Emotions and Senses

LAUREN BRUKNER
ILLUSTRATED BY APSLEY

Jessica Kingsley *Publishers*
London and Philadelphia

First published in 2017
by Jessica Kingsley Publishers
73 Collier Street
London N1 9BE, UK
and
400 Market Street, Suite 400
Philadelphia, PA 19106, USA

www.jkp.com

Library of Congress Cataloging in Publication Data
Names: Brukner, Lauren. | Apsley, illustrator.
Title: Stay cool and in control with the keep-calm guru : wise ways for
  children to regulate their emotions and senses / Lauren Brukner ;
  illustrated by Apsley.
Description: Philadelphia : Jessica Kingsley Publishers, 2016. | Audience:
  Age: 7-14.
Identifiers: LCCN 2016015826 | ISBN 9781785927140 (alk. paper)
Subjects: LCSH: Emotions in children--Juvenile literature. | Yoga--Juvenile
  literature. | Child psychology--Juvenile literature.
Classification: LCC BF723.E6 B785 2016 | DDC 155.4/124--
dc23 LC record available at https://lccn.loc.gov/2016015826

British Library Cataloguing in Publication Data
A CIP catalogue record for this book is available from the British Library

ISBN 978 1 78592 714 0
eISBN 978 1 78450 300 0

Printed and bound in the United States

This book is dedicated to all children.

I truly believe that each and every one of you has a beautiful, unique, and special spark of inner peace, beauty, warmth, light, and strength that glows within your heart.

Sometimes, when it feels the most dark, it is then that you have the chance to prove to yourselves just how brightly that light can shine; and you realize, in those moments, how much your light can not only illuminate your life, but your own piece of the world.

Contents

PART 1: FOR KIDS   **9**

1. Meet the Keep-Calm Guru   11

2. What Is Your Light?   13

3. The Mind-Body Connection   16

4. The Big Four: Just Right, Slow and Tired, Fast and Emotional, and Fast and Wiggly   18

5. Making Abstract Feelings Tangible   24

6. Specific Steps to Get to that "Just Right" Feeling   29

7. How this Book Works   31

8. Anywhere Body Breaks: The Science Behind the What and the Why   33

9. Anywhere Body Breaks: The Science Behind the How   37

10. Tools: Using the Stuff Most of You (Probably) Already Have   64

11. Big Body Breaks: Or Shall We Say, Yoga   87

12. The End of Our Journey—For Now   100

13. Sum it Up   101

PART 2: FOR ADULTS

105

Acknowledgements

106

For Parents and Caregivers—How to Get the Most Out of This
Book

108

For Teachers and Therapists—How to Get the Most Out of This
Book

110

Maslow's Hierarchy of Human Needs, and its Connection to
Child Development

112

Simple Supports to Promote Overall Self-Regulation

116

Appendix 1: "Just Right" Checklist

120

Appendix 2: "My List of Ten" Card

122

Appendix 3: Positive Affirmations

124

Appendix 4: "Just Right" Self-Monitoring Checklist

126

Appendix 5: At a Glance Desk Strip Reminders—Anywhere
Body Breaks, Tools, and Big Breaks/Yoga

128

Appendix 6: At a Glance Bracelet Reminders (for Anywhere
Body Breaks Only)

132

Appendix 7: "Draw and Jot" Journaling Card

135

PART 1

FOR KIDS

CHAPTER 1

Meet the Keep-Calm Guru

Namaste. My name is Aurora. My parents have frequently told the story—on warm summer nights, roasting marshmallows over an open fire, on cold winter mornings, with visiting friends as we hike through the woods around our cottage, the crunch of snow under our boots—that on the day that I was born, the moment that I opened my eyes, it was as if the sun shone through them into their hearts.

That is why they named me Aurora—for light. I believe that there is a light, an ability to achieve peace and serenity that shines through every heart that I connect with. I have spent so much of my life helping others find that light for themselves, most especially when they feel that there is only darkness.

Won't you come on this journey with me? Let's expand on your light, let it shine through your eyes, through your heart, so that even when you have a moment, a day, a week, or more that feels difficult, you can call on that light to warm you, and guide you through that hard time.

For the purpose of this book, and during my work as your mentor during our journey, you may call me by my teacher name, as you are to be my student, yes? I am known as **Keep-Calm Guru**, or, if you would prefer, **Guru Aurora**.

I am so pleased to begin our journey together…

CHAPTER 2

What Is Your Light?

Before we go any further on this wonderful journey of discovering the secrets to serenity, self-control, and peace, it is important for us to truly understand the meaning of what we call **light**.

The idea of light is not a scientific term, like so much that we describe in this book. It does not involve the physical senses, and cannot be measured or quantified. That does not make it any less real, at least to me.

I believe that every person on this earth is born with a spark, a beautiful light that shines within their heart, that allows them to feel in control of the overwhelmingly difficult feelings they may experience throughout their lives, both in their minds and in their hearts.

Someone's light is not always easy to find—especially when they are going through extremely tough times that occur so often in life. Sadly, a person's light can therefore remain buried and hidden.

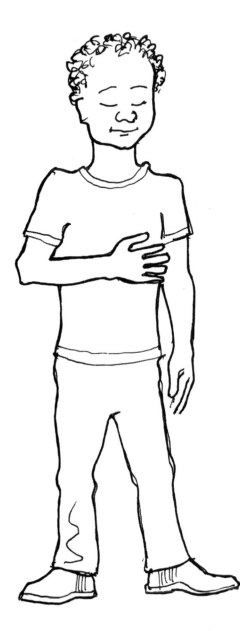

Close your eyes for a moment. Place your hand over your heart. Feel it pulsating under your hand. Do you feel its familiar beat?

Picture a warm light emanating from your heart and through your fingertips. What color is it? What color best represents who you are? Take a moment here. It will come to you.

Your light represents all of your hopes, positive feelings, and beautiful thoughts.

Your light shines brightly when you feel happy, peaceful, content, attentive, and **Just Right**.

Sometimes, it takes some *dark times* (or difficult thoughts or feelings) to bring that light to the surface, and make it shine brightest.

Use those moments as opportunities to be a positive influence on the world.

CHAPTER 3

The Mind-Body Connection

I have written this book together with my friend, Lauren, who is an occupational therapist. We have come together to blend our knowledge of how to connect the mind and body so that you can feel your light shine most brightly.

Many times, we think or feel strong feelings in our hearts, minds, or both, don't we? Examples of this include frustration, anger, sadness, and fear. The problem comes when we don't know what to do with those feelings. They are there, yes? But what should we do with them? They are not tangible—there is nothing to hold on to, correct? That can be quite frustrating.

Other times, we may experience difficult physical feelings. Examples of this may be exhaustion, jumpiness, or wiggliness. When we engage in a physical exercise alone in order to help us feel **Just Right** and back in control, we often find that it's not enough. Ask yourself this question, my students, my friends—are you thinking of how you are feeling before engaging in that exercise?

This is where the importance of the **Mind-Body Connection** comes into play. It is important to link our physical exercises and emotional feelings together to most effectively feel calm and let our light shine through. This allows us to then feel most grounded to our own bodies, to our thoughts, and to where we are in the moment.

We will learn more about this in the following chapters.

CHAPTER 4

The Big Four
Just Right, Slow and Tired, Fast and Emotional, and Fast and Wiggly

It's important to think specifically about *how* we are feeling, and, if we need to get back in control of either our body, mind, or heart, to then choose the **Just Right** strategy or **tool** that helps us stay calm, in control, and filled with light and happiness. This is no easy feat, especially when we are in the heat of a strong physical or emotional reaction. Learning how to label our feelings and use strategies or tools before we get to that point is so important—to try to avoid getting to that point!

Just Right

Just like when our body is cold, goose bumps on our skin emerge automatically in order to help maintain our body's natural temperature, so, too, we find a similar phenomenon with our emotional and physical systems. When we are feeling a strong *physical* or *emotional* feeling that is so intense that it is preventing us from completing what we want or need to do, that is when we are not **Just Right** and our body works hard to get us back to that state (as we will soon see).

Examples of feelings that fall under the category of being **Just Right** include:

Calm	Attentive
Peaceful	Thoughtful
Focused	Pensive
Happy	

Slow and Tired

When we are **Slow and Tired**, this means that we are *so exhausted* that we are unable to complete a task or participate in an activity that we want or need to do. Our eyes may feel droopy, our limbs may feel heavy, it may be hard to sit up, and it may be difficult to focus. We may feel irritated, or cranky. Activities that usually take a short amount of time may take longer because we are so sleepy.

Ask yourself this question, and answer it honestly, my friends: are you getting enough sleep? What time are you getting to bed? If you are having difficulty sleeping, the "deep breathing" exercise introduced later in the book would be a good one to try once you get into bed.

Fast and Emotional

When we are **Fast and Emotional**, this means that we are experiencing such an intense *emotional* feeling in our hearts and our heads that we are unable to complete a task or participate in an activity that we want or need to do.

Examples of feelings that fall under the category of **Fast and Emotional** include, but are not limited to:

Frustrated   Scared

Angry   Jealous

Worried   Overwhelmed

Sad   Overly-excited

Furious

Fast and Wiggly

When we are **Fast and Wiggly**, this means that we are experiencing such an intense *physical* feeling in our bodies that we are unable to complete a task or participate in an activity that we want or need to do.

Examples of feelings that fall under the category of **Fast and Wiggly** include, but are not limited to:

Overwhelming feeling of needing to jump out of our seat

Not feeling where our body is

Hearing too much

Seeing too much

Feeling like we will jump out of our skin

Can you relate to these feelings? I can. I have felt all of these feelings at one point or another. Wait, what did you say, Lauren? Oh—she says that she has, too. She just wanted you to know that.

In the next chapter we will learn the specific steps to getting to that **Just Right** feeling, where you will feel in control of your emotions, your body, and your heart. Where your light can shine through beautifully and comfortingly.

OK, my students. Let us move on.

CHAPTER 5

Making Abstract Feelings Tangible

That's a mouthful, isn't it? When we are talking about feelings, I thought it would be important to take a pause, and really understand how to go about not only exploring, but also personalizing our own versions of **Slow and Tired**, **Fast and Emotional**, and **Fast and Wiggly** feelings. We are all on a journey of exploring our inner selves. Just as my favorite song may differ from yours, my version of **Fast and Emotional** feelings will most certainly also differ.

In order to make what we feel less abstract (or not able to be easily understood), and more real or tangible, we need to accomplish two things:

1. Picture and understand where we feel the feeling/s in our body.

2. See, or visualize, what the feeling/s look like. We will accomplish this by picturing our feelings through colors.

Let us begin.

Slow and Tired

★ Close your eyes.

★ Where do you generally feel the group of **Slow and Tired** feelings in your body? Do you feel them in one place, such as behind your eyes? In two places, such as your brain and your back? Do you have this group of feelings all across your body? Take a moment to think about where you usually have this group of feelings.

★ With your eyes closed, we are going to focus on the color, or colors, of this group of feelings. Are they red? Blue, mixed with purple? Take a moment to picture the color/s of these **Slow and Tired** feelings.

★ Great. Now we have a visual of our feelings to work with, correct? Keep that visual in your mind. You now have two choices here:

   – *Physically* take these **Slow and Tired** feelings in your hands, from whichever places in your body they stem from, picturing their color/s clearly in your mind. Squash or squeeze them until they disappear, or at least become manageable for you to move on with your day.

   – *Mentally* take these **Slow and Tired** feelings from wherever in your body they stem from, picturing their color/s clearly in your mind. Squash or squeeze them, using the power of your imagination, until they disappear, or at least become manageable for you to move on with your day.

We will explore *what* **Anywhere Body Breaks** are, and *why* they are so beneficial to us, in Chapter 8. We will then learn the *how*, the actual ways to complete **Anywhere Body Breaks**, in Chapter 9.

Fast and Emotional

 Close your eyes.

 Where do you generally feel the group of **Fast and Emotional** feelings in your body? Do you feel them in one place, such as your stomach? In two places, such as your head and neck? Do you have this group of feelings all across your body? Take a moment to think about where you usually have this group of feelings.

 With your eyes closed, we are going to focus on the color, or colors, of this group of feelings. Are they green? Orange, mixed with yellow? Take a moment to picture the color/s of these **Fast and Emotional** feelings.

 Great. Now we have a visual of our feelings to work with:

- *Physically* take these **Fast and Emotional** feelings in your hands, from whichever places in your body they stem from, picturing their color/s clearly in your mind. Squash or squeeze them until they disappear, or at least become manageable for you to move on with your day.

- *Mentally* take these **Fast and Emotional** feelings, from wherever in your body they stem from, picturing their color/s clearly in your mind. Squash or squeeze them, using the power of your imagination, until they disappear, or at least become manageable for you to move on with your day.

We will explore *what* **Anywhere Body Breaks** are, and *why* they are so beneficial to us, in Chapter 8. We will then learn the *how*, the actual ways to complete **Anywhere Body Breaks**, in Chapter 9.

Fast and Wiggly

★ Close your eyes.

★ Where do you generally feel the group of **Fast and Wiggly** feelings in your body? Do you feel them in one place, such as your brain? In two places, such as your arms and legs? Do you have this group of feelings all across your body? Take a moment to think about where you usually have this group of feelings.

★ With your eyes closed, we are going to focus on the color, or colors, of this group of feelings. Are they red? Brown, mixed with gold? Take a moment to picture the color/s of these **Fast and Wiggly** feelings.

★ Great. Now we have a visual of our feelings to work with:

- *Physically* take these **Fast and Wiggly** feelings in your hands, from whichever places in your body they stem from, picturing their color/s clearly in your mind. Squash or squeeze them until they disappear, or at least become manageable for you to move on with your day.

- *Mentally* take these **Fast and Wiggly** feelings, from whichever places in your body they stem from, picturing their color/s clearly in your mind. Squash or squeeze them, using the power of your imagination, until they disappear, or at least become manageable for you to move on with your day.

We will explore *what* **Anywhere Body Breaks** are, and *why* they are so beneficial to us, in Chapter 8. We will then learn the *how*, the actual ways to complete **Anywhere Body Breaks**, in Chapter 9.

In the next chapter we will be learning the first step in understanding and gaining control of our feelings: a simple yet very important checklist that, with routine practice, should really improve your ability to gain a better sense of your own thoughts, emotions, and ability to do what you need to and want to do in your daily life. Sounds intriguing? It's called...drum roll please...**The "Just Right" Checklist**. I know, it doesn't sound flashy or too exciting, but it's a game-changer, I promise.

CHAPTER 6

Specific Steps to Get to that "Just Right" Feeling

I have found (and have been told) in my travels across the globe, meeting with kids, teens, and adults, that having a concrete visual list of steps to gain control and feel calm is helpful. Do you agree? Let us look below at the checklist that I have written over the course of the past few years. This can be downloaded from Appendix 1. ☺

The "Just Right" Checklist

1. **Breathing-Feelings Check-In.** Place one flat palm over your heart, and another over your belly. Pay attention to your breathing as it goes in and out. Is it even, or are you breathing too quickly/too slowly? Feel your heartbeat under your hand. Is it beating evenly, or is it racing? If your breathing and heartbeat is too fast, force yourself to take slow and even breaths (read the next chapter for detailed instructions on **Bubble Breath with Forced Exhalation**). You can always try this strategy to check in and see how your body is responding to a feeling, or to try to even out your breathing and heart rate, when you

are feeling **Slow and Tired**, **Fast and Emotional**, or **Fast and Wiggly**.

2. **Label your feeling/s.** Now that you have slowed down your breathing, you have allowed enough oxygen to enter your brain and given yourself time to think. How are you feeling? Think of the category first (**Fast and Emotional**, etc.). Picture where in your body your feeling is, and the color/s of this feeling. Then go more specifically (i.e. are you frustrated, sad, etc.).

3. **Connect your feeling to your strategy.** Think of your feeling. Take the feeling in your hand, as if it were physical. Now, whatever strategy you choose (and we will go into more detail in the following chapters), take the energy of that feeling and make it disappear through the use of the physical, tangible exercise or use of a **tool**. This step directly relates to the idea of the **Mind-Body Connection**.

Feeling/s: _____

Strategy/ies: _____

Does this checklist make the process of calming down clearer? We will review it again once we delve into specific exercises and tools. I applaud your hard work and willingness to be the best people you can be.

In the next chapter we will learn how this book will act like a manual for you, a quick user-friendly guide for you, my students, to be able to manage these feelings and to let your beautiful light shine through calmly and happily.

CHAPTER 7

How this Book Works

This is where I, as your teacher and guru, become excited. This is the turning point in the book, kind students. This is the part of the book where you begin to take the reins on your own feelings.

Each category of feelings is represented by a symbol.

This symbol represents the category of **Slow and Tired**, and feelings under its umbrella. So whenever you see this symbol next to any exercise or **tool**, you will know immediately that those strategies will help if you are feeling this way.

This symbol represents the category of **Fast and Emotional**, and feelings under its umbrella. So whenever you see this symbol next to any exercise or **tool**, you will know immediately that those strategies will help if you are feeling this way.

This symbol represents the category of **Fast and Wiggly**, and feelings under its umbrella. So whenever you see this symbol next to any exercise or **tool**, you will know immediately that those strategies will help if you are feeling this way.

This is so important—and what makes this book really like a manual for you, readers—when you see one of these symbols next to a strategy or

tool, that means that the strategy or **tool** can help with that feeling. Got it? ☺

In the next chapter, we will explore something called **Anywhere Body Breaks**—small exercises that you can do anywhere to help keep you calm, content, and **Just Right**.

We will learn the science behind how and why they work, as inquiring minds want to know, am I right? Plus, once we are able to understand how they work, this will be helpful in keeping us doing the exercises—am I right?

CHAPTER 8

Anywhere Body Breaks
The Science Behind the What and the Why

The what and the why...

An **Anywhere Body Break** is a *small movement* exercise that you can do *using your own body*. The reason I call it "small movement" is because you can do these exercises from a regular sitting or standing stance, *without having to change your whole body position*. They work really well, and the great news is that you can use them without disrupting what you were doing to either get a **tool** (don't worry, we'll get there) or take a **Big Break** (we'll get there too). There is one important factor to note.

Mindset: Think back to our process of getting to **Just Right**. There is a certain process to follow, remember? We have the **Breathing-Feelings Check-In** → **Label your feelings** → **Connect the feeling to the strategy**. It is important to have the correct *mindset* when completing an **Anywhere Body Break**, or it will not be effective. We have to take our strategies seriously, as we are mature students and individuals on a quest to gain self-control, yes?

The how

I do not apologize for getting slightly scientific with you, my enlightened friends. Understanding the science behind what we are learning only helps motivate us, and involves us as teachers as well, no? One of the ways that **Anywhere Body Breaks** work to get our bodies to **Just Right** is by acting on our nervous systems in the brain.

When we are experiencing a heightened physical or emotional feeling, our body goes into what is called *fight or flight*. This is done by our *sympathetic nervous system.* It is an automatic response to get us out of danger, and dates back to long ago, to when we lived in caves, and had real, daily dangerous encounters that required quick *fight or flight* reactions. What would you do if a sabretooth tiger showed up at the front of your cave? You would need to be prepared, yes? Your eyes would dilate to see better, you may start sweating, ready to run at a second's notice, your digestion may slow, your head may be pounding with all that extra blood flowing.

Do any of these physical symptoms sound familiar? Even though (we hope) we don't have any sabretooth tigers visiting our homes, we may have similar reactions to significantly less-threatening events that happen in our lives. That's our *sympathetic nervous system* trying to protect us.

What do we do, you may ask. We have to activate the *parasympathetic nervous system*, of course! It is responsible for countering the effects of the *sympathetic nervous system.*

Guess what? Many of the **Anywhere Body Breaks** that we will talk about involve different physical movements that activate the *parasympathetic nervous system*—our hero!

Here are some examples of movements that **Anywhere Body Breaks** use that activate the *parasympathetic nervous system*:

★ **Deep breathing (with forced exhalation).** One of the quickest ways to get our bodies back into that **Just Right** and peaceful place and out of *fight or flight* is by taking a good deep breath. We are going to learn a specific type of deep breathing, where the exhale is longer than the inhale, ensuring that it is easier and more effective to get us back into this **Just Right** state.

★ **Proprioception and movements against resistance.** Proprioception means when we give deep pressure and what therapists like Lauren call "input" to the different joints of our bodies. This gives our body information of where it is in space. When you are feeling a strongly negative feeling, whether it is physical or emotional, do you ever just not feel grounded and want to be tightly hugged (whether by a loved one, yourself, or by a ton of blankets)? We have a ton of exercises that will help you feel grounded to yourself, to your center, and to the earth.

★ **Vestibular input.** Lauren is insisting that I use that therapist word again—I apologize for both of us. Your body receives **vestibular input** when you move your head either below your heart, or in a rotational direction. This can be very calming.

★ **Crossing midline.** Your brain is made up of two sides, called the right and left hemispheres. They are responsible for different functions. Sometimes they don't communicate optimally, especially when you are in a *fight or flight* situation. When a part of one side of the body (e.g. an arm) is moved to extend over to the other side of the body, this allows for those two hemispheres, to, well, get back to talking, and for you to get into the **Just Right** position. Many exercises that we will introduce have **crossing midline** elements, don't you worry.

OK, my friends. Now that we are well educated in the what, why, and how of **Anywhere Body Breaks**, we are ready to learn the specific exercises. Let us begin.

CHAPTER 9

Anywhere Body Breaks
The Science Behind the How

BUBBLE BREATH WITH FORCED EXHALATION

This is a good strategy to use whether you are feeling **Slow and Tired**, **Fast and Emotional**, or **Fast and Wiggly**. Getting oxygen to your brain can also help you think better and make smarter choices. The inhale breath is longer than the exhale breath. Try to use this type of breathing when completing your **Breathing-Feelings Check-In**. This is also a good exercise to do before going to bed.

Directions

⭐ Breathe in through your nose slowly for 4 seconds, HOLD, breathe out through your mouth slowly and with control for 6 seconds.

★   Alternatively: Breathe in through your nose slowly for 5 seconds, HOLD, breathe out through your mouth slowly and with control for 7 seconds.

★   Repeat as needed. Gauge how you feel with each breath.

BREATHING-FEELINGS CHECK-IN

This strategy is geared at helping you identify/label your feelings, but can also assist you in evening out your breathing and heart rate, especially when you are **Fast and Emotional** or **Fast and Wiggly**.

Directions

★ Close your eyes.

★ Put one hand on your heart and one hand on your belly.

★ Pay attention to your breathing in your belly as it goes in and out. Is it even, or are you breathing too quickly/ too slowly?

★ Feel your heartbeat under your hand. Is it beating evenly, or is it racing?

★ If your breathing and heartbeat is too fast, force yourself to take slow and even breaths.

★ Now that you have slowed down your breathing, you have allowed enough oxygen to enter your brain and given yourself time to think. How are you feeling? Think of the category first (**Fast and Emotional**, etc.). Picture where in your body your feeling is, and the color/s of this feeling. Then go more specifically (i.e. are you frustrated, sad, etc.). Label your feeling.

DEEP PRESSURE LEG MASSAGE

Deep Pressure Leg Massage can help you feel where your legs are by giving you **proprioceptive** and **vestibular input**, which can then help calm you down whether you are feeling **Fast and Emotional** or **Fast and Wiggly**. It can also wake you up if you are feeling **Slow and Tired**.

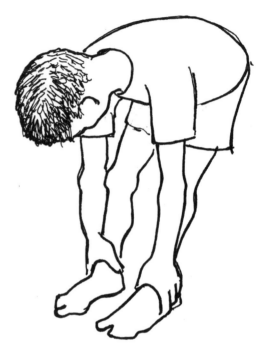

Directions

★ Label your feeling/s. Connect your feeling/s to the **Deep Pressure Leg Massage** exercise.

★ Put the feeling/s in the palms of your hands.

★ Reach down, place your hands either around your ankles or on the top of your thighs.

★ Rub up from the ankles, or down from the thighs, slowly and with firm pressure.

★ Repeat 3–5 times, until the feeling/s disappear.

FIND YOUR LIGHT

Your light shines brightly when you feel happy, peaceful, content, attentive, and **Just Right**. Sometimes, it takes some *dark times* (or difficult thoughts or feelings) to bring that light to the surface, and make it shine brightest. This is a good exercise to use when you are feeling **Fast and Emotional**.

Directions

★ Label your feeling/s. Connect the feeling/s to the **Finding Your Light** exercise.

★ Place the feelings in the palm of your hand.

★ Close your eyes for a moment.

★ Place your hand over your heart. Feel it pulsating under your hand. Do you feel its familiar beat?

★ Picture a warm light emanating from your heart, and through your fingertips.

★ What color is it? What color best represents who you are? Take a moment here. It will come to you.

★ Your light represents all of your hopes, positive feelings, and beautiful thoughts.

★ As you let the warmth of this light come through your hand, let it erase the feelings you had through its brightness.

HAND RUB

Hand Rub can help you feel where your arms are by giving you **proprioceptive input**, which can then help calm you down, whether you are feeling **Fast and Emotional** or **Fast and Wiggly**. It can also wake you up if you are feeling **Slow and Tired**.

Directions

★ Label your feeling/s. Take the feeling/s into the **Hand Rub** exercise.

★ Put the feeling/s under your thumb. Starting with one thumb, rub firmly around the perimeter of the opposite palm 5–10 times.

★ Repeat with the other palm, until the feeling/s disappear.

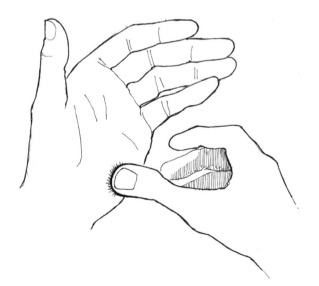

WRIST CROSS

Wrist Cross can help you feel where your wrists and hands are by giving you **proprioceptive input**, while also **crossing midline** (which is great for focusing and calming!). This exercise is great whether you are **Fast and Emotional** or **Fast and Wiggly**. It can also wake you up if you are feeling **Slow and Tired**.

Directions

★ Label your feeling/s. Take the feeling/s into the **Wrist Cross** exercise.

★ Cross your wrists together, with the inside of one wrist pressing against the back of the other. Place your feeling/s between your wrists.

★ Push them firmly together, and hold this position for at least 5–10 seconds. Push that feeling between your wrists until it disappears.

LEG CROSS

Leg Cross can help you feel where your legs are by giving you **proprioceptive input**, while also **crossing midline** (which is great for focusing and calming). This exercise is great whether you are **Fast and Emotional** or **Fast and Wiggly**. It can also wake you up if you are feeling **Slow and Tired**.

Directions

★ Label your feeling/s. Take the feeling/s into the **Leg Cross** exercise.

★ Cross your legs together, with the inside of one leg pressing against the top of the other. Place the feeling in between.

★ Push your legs firmly together, and hold this position for at least 5–10 seconds. Squeeze the feeling until it disappears.

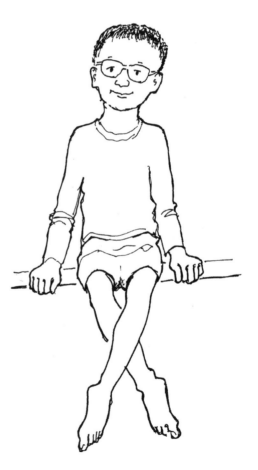

POSITIVE SELF-TALK/ AFFIRMATIONS

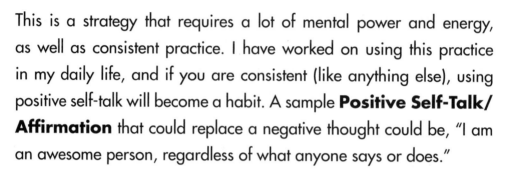

This is a strategy that requires a lot of mental power and energy, as well as consistent practice. I have worked on using this practice in my daily life, and if you are consistent (like anything else), using positive self-talk will become a habit. A sample **Positive Self-Talk/ Affirmation** that could replace a negative thought could be, "I am an awesome person, regardless of what anyone says or does."

Other sample positive affirmations could be:

"The glass is half full."

"I can't change other people—just myself."

"I make my part of the world a better place just by being in it."

"I am confident."

"I know myself as a person and as a learner."

"I can do anything I put my mind to."

"I am fearless."

"I have self-control."

"I love myself for who I am."

"I am focused."

"I am a valuable member of my community."

You can also make up your own—think of motivational sayings that you have heard from loved ones that have resonated with you. Repeat them on a daily basis, even when you are feeling happy.

This strategy is especially great when you are feeling **Fast and Emotional**, and even **Fast and Wiggly**.

Directions

★ Label your feeling/s. Take that feeling into the **Positive Self-Talk/Affirmations** exercise.

★ Which of these statements speaks to you? Do you have any others that you like better? Choose one, or a few, now. Speak them out loud, quietly, or to yourself.

★ Think of a time or an event that validates these affirmations for you. For example, I can think back to entering a room full of people who I didn't know with my head held high, and introducing myself with confidence, even though it took courage on my part. It was hard for me, but I did it. That is the specific situation that I think of when I say "I am confident."

★ As you say the affirmation, feel the words wash over you, erasing any negative feeling you had before.

★ Think of a time of day where you can routinely say one/a few positive affirmations, in order to make it part of your daily life. This will help to make it a habit.

★ Once this becomes a habit, it can help replace negative thoughts with positive self-talk and these specific positive affirmations. ☺

★ Alternatively: Laminate and cut out a card that you can download from Appendix 3. Look over the list. Think over what they mean to you. Are there any others that a loved one or trusted teacher or therapist has said to you that you can add in the blank space? If so, do.

You can also cut out another card, and place it in a visible location in your bedroom, work area, or chill out area, if you have one (we will get into that in the next section).

Note: In Appendix 3 (downloadable) there are cards that can be cut out and laminated to be added to a portable keyring that you can put in your pocket and bring with you anywhere you go. One card has some of the above positive affirmations, with blank spaces for you to add your own. ☺

PROGRESSIVE MUSCLE RELAXATION

This is an exercise where you tense and relax different joints and muscle groups in your body. It gives you that **proprioceptive input**, because it tells you where your body is in space, and is great when you are feeling **Fast and Emotional**, because it is a great stress buster.

Directions

★ Label your feeling/s. Take the feeling/s into the **Progressive Muscle Relaxation** exercise.

★ Put the feeling/s first into your shoulders. Tense them. Hold the position for 5 seconds, then release.

★ Do the same for the wrists, fingers, knees, ankles, and toes. Now the feeling/s should have disappeared.

HAND HOLD

Hand Hold provides **crossing midline** and **proprioceptive inputs**, so it is great when you are feeling **Slow and Tired**, **Fast and Emotional**, and **Fast and Wiggly**.

Directions

★ Label your feeling/s. Take the feeling/s into the **Hand Hold** exercise.

★ Place your palms together.

★ Cross the thumbs.

★ Press and squeeze the feeling/s—hold your own hands together tightly until the feeling/s disappear.

★ Repeat as needed.

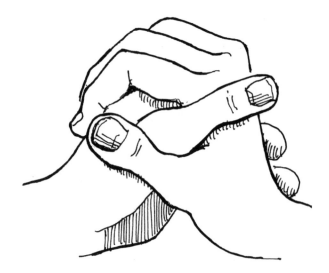

EAR MASSAGE

Providing deep pressure to the lobes of your ears simultaneously gives your body **proprioceptive input,** and allows for increased blood flow to your brain, as well. This is a good exercise to try if you are feeling **Slow and Tired** or **Fast and Emotional**.

Directions

★ Label your feeling/s. Connect your feelings/s to the **Ear Massage** exercise.

★ Take your feeling, and place it between both thumbs and index fingers of your hands.

★ Starting from the top of your ears, gently pull your ears outwards and rub downwards towards the fleshy lobes of your ears (if you are wearing earrings, go around them).

★ As you slowly rub down your ears, picture the feeling disappearing.

FEEL WHERE YOUR BODY IS

When we feel a strong **Fast and Emotional** or **Fast and Wiggly** feeling, and begin to enter *fight or flight*, it can be difficult to feel all the different parts of our body. Doing this exercise correctly is very calming, because it tells each of the joints of our body where they are through **proprioceptive input**, and relaxes our nervous system.

Directions

★ Label your feeling/s. Connect your feeling/s to the **Feel Where Your Body Is** exercise.

★ Place your feeling/s in your palms.

★ Cross your hands over your shoulders and gently squeeze. Quietly say to yourself, "Here are my shoulders."

★ Move down to your elbows—cross your hands over your elbows and gently squeeze. Quietly say to yourself, "Here are my elbows."

★ Move down to your wrists—cross your hands over your wrists and gently squeeze. Quietly say to yourself, "Here are my wrists."

★ Move down to your right hand—go to each finger and gently squeeze with your left hand. Quietly say to yourself, "Here is my pinky. Here is my ring finger. Here is my middle finger. Here is my pointer. Here is my thumb."

★ Move down to your left hand—go to each finger and gently squeeze with your right hand. Quietly say to yourself, "Here is my pinky. Here is my ring finger. Here is my middle finger. Here is my pointer. Here is my thumb."

★ Move down to your hips—cross your hands over your hips and gently squeeze. Quietly say to yourself, "Here are my hips."

★ Move down to your knees—cross your hands over your knees and gently squeeze. Quietly say to yourself, "Here are my knees."

★ Move down to your ankles—cross your hands over your ankles and gently squeeze. Quietly say to yourself, "Here are my ankles."

★ Move down to your feet—cross your hands over your feet and gently squeeze. Quietly say to yourself, "Here are my feet."

★ Alternatively: Stand straight and tall (good posture, right?). Taking a deep breath in, bend down and squeeze your ankles with both hands, with an exhaled breath out. With each body part, name it. For example, after the ankles, move up and squeeze your knees, breathing in and out, and saying "knees." Move up to the hips, firmly squeezing your hips, breathing in and out, saying "hips." Finally, move up to the shoulders, feeling the shoulders, breathing in and out, saying "shoulders."

ARM TAPS

This is an alerting activity, and is great if you are feeling **Slow and Tired**. By tapping your body, you are giving it awareness of where it is in space. Since we are crossing our arms, we are **crossing midline**, so this is also an alerting exercise. Please use good body control, and don't tap too hard!

Directions

★ Label your feeling/s. Connect your feeling/s to this **Arm Taps** exercise.

★ Place your feeling/s under each palm of both hands.

★ Cross your arms, placing each palm on the top of the opposite shoulders.

★ Making your way down each arm, firmly (but not too firmly!) tap the feeling/s away until they disappear.

EYE PALMING

This exercise is a nice way to relax and take a moment to yourself and block out everything that you see, especially if you are feeling overwhelmed (physically or emotionally). It is a nice one to try if you are feeling **Fast and Emotional** or **Fast and Wiggly**.

Directions

★ Label your feeling/s. Connect your feeling/s to this **Eye Palming** exercise.

★ Put your feeling/s in between both palms. Rub them together briskly until they feel warm.

★ Gently place your warmed palms over your eyes, breathing in and out slowly, letting the darkness settle over you, feeling the warmth of your hands over your eyes, letting the feeling/s slowly disappear.

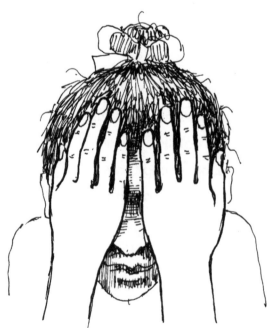

LEG TAPS

This is an alerting activity, and is great if you are feeling **Slow and Tired**. By tapping your body, you are giving your body awareness of where it is in space. Since we are crossing our arms across our body, we are **crossing midline**, so this is also an alerting exercise. Please use good body control, and don't tap too hard!

Directions

★ Label your feeling/s. Connect your feeling/s to the **Leg Taps** exercise.

★ Place your feeling/s under each palm of both hands.

★ Cross your arms, placing each palm on the top of the opposite thighs, near the hips.

★ Making your way down each thigh, firmly (but not too firmly!) tap the feeling/s away until they disappear.

INVERT YOUR HEAD

Inverting your head provides you with **vestibular input**, which is calming. As soon as you feel your own personal "alarm bells" of *fight or flight*, why don't you simply try inverting your head? This simply means giving yourself a dose of **vestibular input**. This is a good exercise to try when you are feeling **Fast and Emotional**.

Important: Ask a doctor or parent/guardian if there is any medical reason that you are not able to do this (it has to do with blood flow).

Directions

★ Label your feeling/s. Take the feeling/s into this exercise of **Inverting Your Head**.

★ Visualize where your feelings are—picture them in your head. As you lower your head, picture the feelings leaving your body and disappearing.

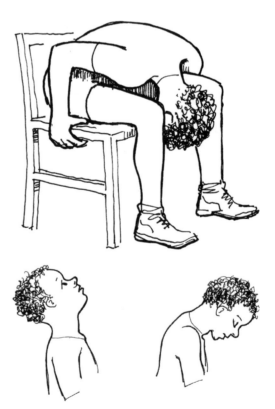

Examples of ways to invert your head, or to give yourself **vestibular input**, include:

★ Reaching down to get something from the floor

★ Rolling your neck back and forth

★ Rolling your neck in a rotational manner

★ Putting your head between your knees

MINFULNESS

This is a simple exercise where you take time to stop, turn inwards, block out the world that is continuing to go on around you, and focus on how you are feeling. There are many ways to use this practice. **Mindfulness** is a good practice to build into your daily routine to help you keep your light shining, and feeling happy and in control. It is a good strategy to use if you are feeling **Fast and Emotional** or **Fast and Wiggly**. One simple way is as follows:

Directions

★ Label your feeling/s. Connect your feeling/s to the **Mindfulness** exercise.

★ Set a timer starting at one minute. Place one hand on your heart, and one hand on your belly.

★ Tell yourself the following: "For this one minute, I am going to focus only on my breathing, noticing how it goes in, noticing how it goes out. If any thought

comes, I can acknowledge it, let it float away, and re-focus on my breathing."

★ Once you are successfully able to focus on your breathing for one minute, slowly add time to the timer (for example, in 15–30 second increments).

CHAPTER 10

Tools

Using the Stuff Most of You (Probably) Already Have

You have learned much already, my students. Even with the knowledge of the **Anywhere Body Breaks** that you have studied, you could happily and successfully get through many days, I think. **Tools** are important, too, and they have their place in our daily lives. If you look around you, I think that you would see that many people already use them without realizing it.

It is with the knowledge of what everyday objects are for, and how they can help us, that we can use them that more efficiently, don't you think?

Let us very briefly go into what our definition of a **tool** is.

A **tool** is a physical, tangible object that can help its user organize, calm, and re-focus the mind and body. Just like with the **Anywhere Body Breaks**, it is important to have that **Mind-Body Connection**, and to go through the same checklist for the **Breathing-Feelings Check-In**:

The "Just Right" Checklist

1. **Breathing-Feelings Check-In**. Place one flat palm over your heart, and another over your belly. Pay attention to your breathing as it goes in and out. Is it even, or are you breathing too quickly/too slowly? Feel your heartbeat under your hand. Is it beating evenly, or is it racing? If your breathing and heartbeat is too fast, force yourself to take slow and even breaths. You can always try this strategy to check in and see how your body is responding to a feeling, or to try to even out your breathing and heart rate, when you are feeling **Slow and Tired**, **Fast and Emotional**, or **Fast and Wiggly**.

2. **Label your feeling/s.** Now that you have slowed down your breathing, you have allowed enough oxygen to enter your brain and given yourself time to think. How are you feeling? Think of the category first (**Fast and Emotional**, etc.). Then go more specifically (i.e. are you frustrated, sad, etc.). Label your feeling/s.

3. **Connect your feeling to your strategy.** Think of your feeling. Take the feeling in your hand, as if it were physical. Now, whatever strategy you choose (and we will go into detail in the following chapters), take the energy of that feeling and make it disappear through the use of the physical, tangible exercise or **tool**. This step directly relates to the idea of the **Mind-Body Connection**.

   Feeling/s: _____

   Strategy/ies: _____

OK. I believe that we are ready to begin, don't you?

MP3 PLAYER

Upload tracks of binaural beats music to your MP3 player, with a focus on relaxation, creativity, or focus/attention. Thus, when you are feeling **Slow and Tired**, you can use a *focusing/attention* track of music with higher frequencies of music. When you are feeling **Fast and Emotional** or **Fast and Wiggly**, you can use a *relaxation* track with lower frequencies of music.

Binaural beats/tones are tones of slightly different frequencies, presented to each ear. Research has shown that binaural beats can improve attention, creativity, and overall relaxation (depending on the tone). You can upload binaural beats music (e.g. Hemi-Sync®) directly to your MP3 player.

MY LIST OF TEN

Everybody has strengths, and things that they need to work on. Some days feel harder than others, and this is a great **tool** if you are feeling **Fast and Emotional** and need a boost in your confidence.

My List of 10
I am a great friend

Directions

★ Label your feeling/s. Take the feeling/s into the use of this **My List of Ten tool**.

★ Come up with ten things that define who you are. Take your time.

★ Think—what makes you special? What makes you unique and amazingly awesome?

★ Write out your list, and attach it to a keyring.

★ You can also cut out another card, and attach it to the surface by your bed, workspace, etc.

★ Look at this list whenever you need a boost! ☺

Note: In Appendix 2 (downloadable), there are cards that can be cut out and laminated to be added to a portable keyring that you can put in your pocket and bring with you anywhere you go. One card has some of the above sayings, with blank spaces for you to add your own. ☺

"DRAW AND JOT" JOURNALING

Hey all, its Lauren here. I wanted to jump in for a second, as this is one of my all-time favorite strategies *ever*, so I definitely wanted to write this strategy down! As a kid, and later as a teenager, I really didn't have the tools or strategies to manage my emotions (and trust me, I was the kind of teen who should have!). Anyway, one outlet that I began to discover on my own was writing (and here I am, a few years later, writing my third book (yes, *Keep-Calm Guru*, co-writing it!). So some of you may be budding writers or artists…anyway, getting off-track here).

Journaling, quickly jotting down a feeling, or simply drawing it out is a great way to vent and get out your feeling. It's also a tangible way to "shut-the-door," so to speak, as you close the cover of the book (giving you a closure of sorts). This is a nice **tool** to use if you are feeling **Fast and Emotional**.

Directions

★ Label your feeling/s. Connect the feeling/s to the use of this **"Draw and Jot" Journaling tool**.

★ If you are using the cards from Appendix 7 (downloadable), laminate 1–3. Attach them to your keyring. Using a thin-tip dry erase marker that you can place in your pocket, this can be a portable "journal-on-the-go."

★ If you are using the sheet templates, on the top of the sheets, they have an option of going through the following process:

- **"Breathing-Feelings Check-In"**

- Label your feeling/s

- Connect your feeling/s to your strategy

- Write/jot/draw it out!

Note: In Appendix 7 (downloadable), there are sheets of different sizes that can be put into a binder and cards that can be cut out and laminated to be added to a portable keyring that you can put in your pocket and bring with you anywhere you go. One card has some of the above sayings, with blank spaces for you to add your own. ☺

YOGA BALL

Sitting on a yoga ball provides you with **vestibular input**, which helps get the *nervous system* out of *fight or flight*—so this can be a good **tool** if you are **Fast and Emotional**. It also can help wake you up if you are **Slow and Tired**.

Directions

★ Label your feeling/s. Connect your feeling/s to the use of the **yoga ball tool.**

★ Be careful when you sit on it—ensure that you are sitting carefully, or you may lose your balance and fall off.

★ Alternatively #1: for increased stability, try putting the yoga ball in a large cardboard box or milk crate. This makes it more like a seat, but still allows you to move around.

★ Alternatively #2: With a controlled body, try lying on your belly on the ball, as long as you can hold yourself steady on the floor with flat palms, and also support yourself with your feet reaching the floor. This position gives you even more **vestibular input**. Make sure that you have enough strength and stability before doing his exercise, and start with having an adult supervise and give you the OK.

WEARABLE FIDGET/RUBBER KEYRING BRACELET

I sometimes find myself fiddling with the elastic of my bracelet during lessons that run especially long. A nice alternative to a standard stress ball would be to get a simple and loose rubber keyring bracelet—the kind that is curled. The texture would

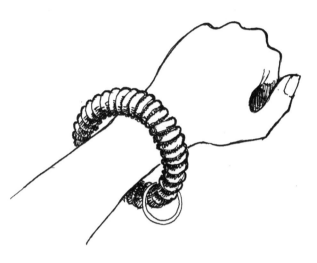

be great if you are feeling **Slow and Tired**, nice to fidget with if you were feeling **Fast and Wiggly** or **Fast and Emotional**, would not be as distracting as a standard fidget, is portable (and just looks like a band that you wear on your wrist!).

Directions

⭐ Label your feeling/s. Connect your feeling/s to the **wearable fidget/rubber keyring bracelet tool**.

⭐ If you are feeling **Slow and Tired**, simply rub the textured surface of the bracelet back and forth, to wake your body up.

⭐ If you are feeling **Fast and Emotional**, pulling it back and forth in a repetitive manner may be helpful. Think of your feelings disappearing with every pull of the bracelet.

★ If you are feeling **Fast and Wiggly**, make an effort to pull or twist on the bracelet (just not too tightly, so you don't hurt yourself!). Try to make the connection that you are touching this fidget bracelet instead of other items, and getting your extra energy out through fidgeting with this **tool**.

SWIVEL CHAIR

Swivel chairs are great for a lot of reasons. They offer a good amount of **vestibular input**, so are calming to the nervous system—good to try if you are feeling **Fast and Emotional**. They can also wake you up if you are **Slow and Tired**, as this type of input serves as alerting. It is important to note that you should be careful with the amount of **vestibular input** you use, as its effect can last for 4–6 hours, and may not show up until later. Do not spin too fast—use self-control and this could be a great seating option for those who need it.

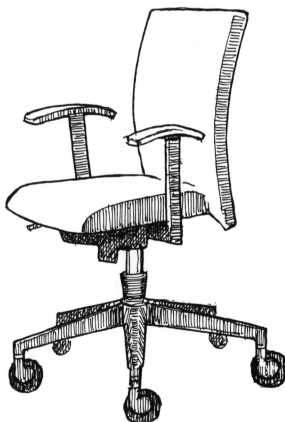

LAUNDRY BASKET STUFFED WITH PILLOWS

Using a large-enough laundry basket with a few pillows provides you with a nice squeeze to your whole body (through **proprioceptive input**). It can be a nice place to read, or do work (just use a clip board!). Depending on your size, this would determine the size of the laundry basket. This would be a good **tool** to use if you are feeling **Slow and Tired**, **Fast and Emotional**, or **Fast and Wiggly**.

INCANDESCENT LIGHTS/ NATURAL LIGHTING

If you are feeling distracted by lots of items on the walls and are bothered by fluorescent lights in the room, ask an adult to replace them with incandescent lights. An incandescent light globe is an electric light that emits a warm glow that is notably less harsh than fluorescent light bulbs (with a fuller spectrum of light). Fluorescent lights emit a poorer quality of light (with a limited spectrum). Lack of exposure to a broad spectrum of lights can affect our bodily functions, such as our circadian rhythm (think sleep!). If this is not an option, try to open blinds and turn off one of the fluorescent lights. This strategy can help if you are feeling **Fast and Emotional** or **Fast and Wiggly**.

LAP PAD/DESK

Do you have any classes that require you to spend a significant amount of time on the floor? Is it hard to take notes and feel where your body is, while staying focused at the same time? If that is the case, you may want to try a lap pad/desk.

Lap pads/desks come in many different shapes, sizes, and textures. For example, some come with soft bottoms, some with weighted bottoms, some have clips on the top, etc.

This would be a good **tool** to use if you are feeling **Slow and Tired** or **Fast and Wiggly**.

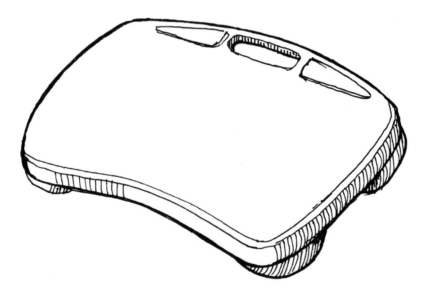

MANDALAS

Did you know that mandalas are a form of meditation? They are a type of coloring page where the design is entirely symmetrical. The level of difficulty goes from simple to extremely intricate. The amount of focus that you need to finish a mandala is complete and all-in. This level of attention needed allows you to take time out of a busy day and to focus entirely on the act of coloring. This is a great activity to complete if you are feeling **Fast and Emotional** or **Fast and Wiggly**.

Note: There are many free downloadable mandalas, with varying levels of difficulty and intricacy, on the internet—just ensure that they are not copyrighted before printing them out. The one below is available to download along with the appendices.

VELCROED EVERYDAY ITEMS

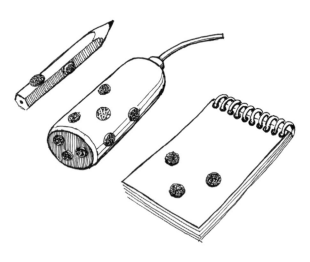

Lauren would like me to say the following to you: "As someone who is frequently tired, I started seeing the value of putting the scratchy Velcro dots on everyday items that I use on a daily basis. *The scratchy Velcro surface acts as alerting tactile (touch) input through receptors in the skin. This really helps me stay awake!* ☺"

This would be a good **tool** to use if you frequently feel **Slow and Tired**, or like to fidget with items—**Fast and Wiggly**. Examples of items where you can place Velcro could be:

★ top of the shaft of a pencil or pen

★ bottom and/or sides of a water bottle with a resistant straw

★ bottom of notebooks/planner

★ bottom of a chair/desk.

BINDER/MULTI-SUBJECT NOTEBOOK

Do you ever feel disorganized—and then worried—with the number of notebooks your teachers give you? I did, when I was your age, and wish I had known this simple organizational secret.

If you have five subjects, buy five different color spiral notebooks (with math being a graph-paper notebook). Buy matching folders with holes. Label them according to the class. Place them into a large, three-ring binder. Once you open the binder, label one pocket, "Place for homework planner," and the other pocket, "Where do I file these papers? Ask a helpful grownup and put away ASAP!"

This is a good **tool** to use if you are feeling generally disorganized, which can result from **Fast and Wiggly** feelings on a routine basis. ☺ Using this system can help you feel less **Fast and Emotional**, as you can more easily find your papers, too!

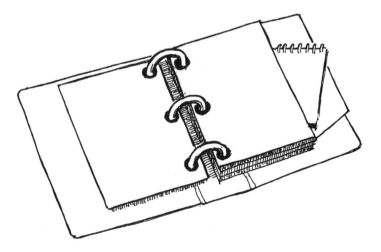

BACKPACK OR BAG

Wearing your backpack or bag frequently and consistently throughout the day, as long as it is heavy enough (but not too heavy that you will hurt your back), will offer a good amount of **proprioceptive input** that should help keep you feeling calm. It's a good **tool** for when you are feeling **Fast and Emotional** or **Fast and Wiggly**.

"HUSBAND" PILLOW

A "husband" pillow, propped up against a hard vertical surface, offers good back support, whether at home or at school, while the arms of the pillow give you additional **proprioceptive input** (as long as it's not too big!). This is a good **tool** to use if you are **Slow and Tired**, **Fast and Emotional**, or **Fast and Wiggly**.

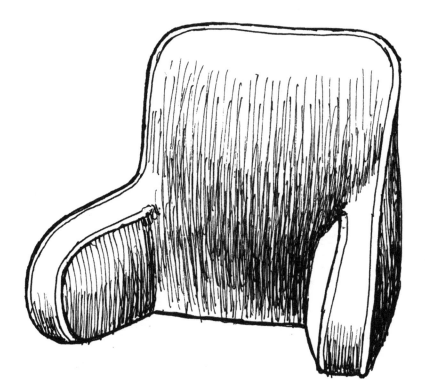

"PET" BED PILLOW

A "pet" bed pillow can offer a good amount of **proprioceptive input**, especially those with raised sides. Just make sure that it's the right fit. Similar to the "husband" pillow, this would be a good option if you are feeling **Slow and Tired**, **Fast and Emotional**, or **Fast and Wiggly**. Don't worry, nobody will think that you are a cat or dog—it looks like a nice pillow! Just don't choose the one with bones or fish heads on it—unless you like those patterns! ☺

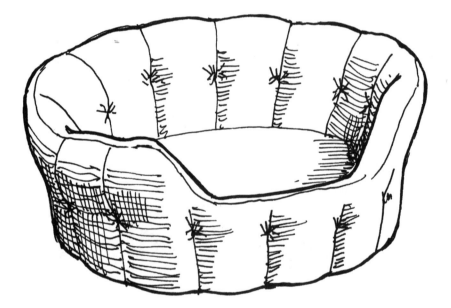

SKETCH THE LESSON

Have you ever felt yourself start to lose focus while a teacher was teaching, and then become worried that you missed the lesson? I have a suggestion for you to try. Ask your teacher if this is a good option to try before beginning, OK? Keeping your hands busy also helps to keep your mind awake. This is a good **tool** to try whether you are **Slow and Tired, Fast and Emotional** (and need to re-focus to the lesson), or **Fast and Wiggly**.

Directions

★ Label your feeling/s, and connect it to the **Sketch the Lesson tool**.

★ Take out either your notebook, binder, or dry erase board and marker.

★ Listen for key words, or the main idea of what the teacher is saying.

★ Sketch your representation of what the teacher is teaching.

★ Figure out a time to share your work with your teacher in advance, and/or participate in the lesson as much as you can!

COOL DOWN/CHILL OUT AREA

A cool down/chill out area is a place to go and cool off when you first start feeling any of those *fight or flight* signs in your body that we spoke about, and when **Anywhere Body Breaks** *are not working well enough.* It is good to use when you are feeling **Fast and Emotional** (where you need to slow down your thoughts) or **Fast and Wiggly** (where you need to slow down your body).

Directions

★ Label your feeling/s. Connect your feeling/s to the use of the cool down/chill out area.

★ You can ask your teachers/therapist/parents to set up a safe spot in your school and/or your house—choose a name for it!

★ It doesn't even have to just be for YOU. (If it's in school, it can kind of be a grade or class-wide cool down/chill out area. In my opinion, every school and home should have one! ☺)

★ You can ask to put in **tools** or items that make you and your peers/siblings feel happy, calm, and safe—letting your light shine through the brightest.

★ Here are some examples to make your cool down/chill out area work well: dim lighting, music player/MP3 player with relaxing music, stress balls, markers/paper, an affirmations list, a "top ten" list, scents of vanilla and lavender (calming), pictures of family/friends, etc. This can always be a safe spot for you (and your classmates/siblings) to go if you begin to feel **Fast and Emotional** or **Fast and Wiggly**.

CHAPTER 11

Big Body Breaks
Or Shall We Say, Yoga

OK, my students, we have learned two out of the three categories of strategies that we will be discussing over this journey. We have talked about "small movement" exercises, or **Anywhere Body Breaks**. We just discussed different types of readily available **tools** to help us feel **Just Right**, happy, and keep our light shining through.

We now explore different "big movement" activities that you can do before and/or after school. Engaging in these activities before school (or at the start of your day in general) can help keep you feeling **Just Right** and happy. Participating in these activities after school (or at the end of the day, regardless) can help make homework, bedtime, and your overall evening easier and more stress-free.

Your choice of times, activity types, and level of activity can depend on what part/s of the day are easiest and most difficult for you, how much time you have, as well as your physical activity capacity; try to schedule these exercises with those factors in mind.

Important: For these exercises, it is best to do them with bare feet and on a yoga mat. Make sure that you have ample floor space to do every pose. Get clearance from parents/guardian and a doctor (if needed) before doing these poses.

DOWNWARD DOG

This exercise provides **proprioceptive input** to your hands, arms, shoulders, and legs, as well as **vestibular input**, so it can make you feel **Just Right**, whether you are feeling **Slow and Tired**, **Fast and Emotional**, or **Fast and Wiggly**.

Directions

★ Label your feeling/s. Connect the feeling/s to your completion of the **Downward Dog** exercise.

★ Place your feeling into the palms of your hands.

★ Lay on your stomach—place flat palms next to your shoulders.

★ Push your body up onto your hands and feet, pushing the feeling under your hands and feet, with legs as straight as you can. Hold for 10 seconds.

★ Repeat until the feeling disappears.

UPWARD FACING DOG

This exercise provides **proprioceptive input** to your belly, back, arms, and legs, and is especially helpful when you are feeling **Slow and Tired** or **Fast and Wiggly**.

Directions

★ Label your feeling/s, and connect the feeling/s to the completion of **Upward Facing Dog** exercise.

★ Place the feeling/s into the palms of your hands.

★ Lay flat on your stomach, palms flat on either side of your chest.

★ Press your body up (placing your feeling under your palms), keeping your knees on the floor, bearing your weight through your palms.

★ Spread your chest, feeling the weight pressing down through your palms. Hold for 10 seconds. Did the feeling disappear? Repeat if it didn't.

BOW POSE

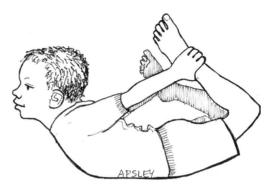

Again, you need enough free floor space to move around in. This exercise provides **proprioceptive input** to the core muscles in your trunk, back, arms, and legs, so it can make you feel **Just Right**, whether you are feeling **Slow and Tired**, **Fast and Emotional**, or **Fast and Wiggly**.

Directions

★ Label your feeling/s. Connect the feelings to use of the **Bow Pose** exercise.

★ Lay on your stomach—bend your knees and lift your feet off the floor.

★ Reach back with your arms to hold your legs right above the ankles (holding the feeling in your hands), lifting your chest off the floor.

★ Push your legs into your hands, as if you are trying to straighten out your legs against your hands. Hold for 5–10 seconds. Did the feeling disappear? Repeat if it didn't.

REVERSE TABLE

Not only does this exercise require a lot of physical strength and endurance, but it also has elements of sustained **proprioceptive** and **vestibular inputs**. It

is a powerful exercise, and can be beneficial if you are feeling **Slow and Tired**, **Fast and Emotional**, or **Fast and Wiggly**.

Directions

★ Label your feeling/s. Connect the feeling/s to the use of the **Reverse Table** exercise.

★ Start by sitting on the floor with your legs extended in front of you and your arms resting at your sides.

★ Place your hands several inches behind your hips, shoulder width apart.

★ Press your palms flat, turning the fingertips inward so that they are pointing in the same direction (toward your toes). Place your feeling under your hands and feet.

★ Firmly plant your hands and feet on the floor, while straightening out your elbows—lift your hips up towards the ceiling.

★ Draw your shoulder blades into your back and lift your chest.

★ Bring your knees, trunk, and chest into a straight line, parallel to the floor.

★ Keep your legs firm, and press down through your toes.

★ If you feel comfortable doing so, carefully and gently drop your head back slightly ("head inversion").

★ Hold for 5–10 seconds. Did the feeling disappear? If not, repeat.

CHILD'S POSE

This position provides both **proprioceptive** and **vestibular inputs**. By curling inwards, you are also offered an opportunity to go inwards and to take a moment for yourself and visually block out the world. This is a good exercise to try if you are feeling **Fast and Emotional** or **Fast and Wiggly**.

Directions

★ Label your feeling/s. Connect the feeling/s to the use of the **Child's Pose** exercise.

★ Start on both knees.

★ Visualize the feeling as at the center of your body. As you move your body inwards, picture the feeling being squeezed away.

★ Bring your bottom towards your heels.

★ Stretch the rest of your body down and forward.

★ Once you are fully stretched, relax your arms along the floor, and rest your stomach along your thighs, with your forehead on the floor or mat.

★ Hold the position for as long as it is comfortable and until the feeling disappears.

SUNRISE, SUNSET

This exercise is completed in standing. You will have to put your head below the level of your knees, while taking deep breaths along with the movements. This provides your body with a significant amount of **vestibular input**. This is a good exercise to try if you are feeling **Slow and Tired**, **Fast and Emotional**, or **Fast and Wiggly**.

Directions

★ Label your feeling/s. Connect your feeling/s to the use of the **Sunrise, Sunset** exercise.

★ Place your feeling/s in the palms of your hands.

★ Lift your hands up to the sky with a deep breath in.

★ With an exhale, reach down to your toes. It's OK if you bend your knees to touch your toes.

★ Repeat, if needed, until the feeling/s disappear.

WINDMILL

This exercise is completed in standing. It requires balance, and you will have to put your head below the level of your knees while turning your neck to look up. This provides your body with a significant amount of **vestibular input**. This is a good exercise to try if you are feeling **Slow and Tired**, **Fast and Emotional**, or **Fast and Wiggly**.

Directions

★ Label your feeling/s. Connect your feeling/s to your **Windmill** exercise.

★ Point your right foot outwards.

★ Place the feeling/s in both hands.

★ With a deep breath in, bend down and touch that foot with the right hand, raising your left arm up.

★ With an exhale, turn your head and look up to the left hand that is pointed upwards.

★ Take a deep breath in, and come back to standing, and exhale. Repeat on the other side.

★ Repeat, until the feeling/s disappear.

KISSING KNEES

This exercise is completed in standing. It requires balance, and you will have to put your head below the level of your knees while turning your neck to look up. This provides your body with a significant amount of **vestibular** and **proprioceptive inputs** (as you squeeze your body inwards). This is a good exercise to try if you are feeling **Slow and Tired**, **Fast and Emotional**, or **Fast and Wiggly**.

Directions

★ Label your feeling/s. Connect your feeling/s to the **Kissing Knees** exercise.

★ Begin in standing position.

★ Place your feeling/s at the tops of your knees.

★ Breathe in, and bend your knees.

★ Fold your body to have your head touch your knees as you exhale.

★ Hold the position for 5–10 seconds, or until the feeling disappears.

CHAPTER 12

The End of Our Journey—For Now

My students! You have done it. You have carefully gone through each page, read through each strategy, and now understand the meaning behind the different exercises and **tools**. I hope that this journey has been enlightening for you, and has put you in the driver's seat of your life when it comes to controlling your own feelings.

You know what's best for you—just like I love veggie burgers, you may love hot dogs. It is the same with strategies, correct? I cannot choose the **Just Right** strategy that will help you feel happy and in control— you have the power because it is your body, your heart.

Choose wisely. Our journey, through the pages of this book, has given you the **tools** and power to do this. Be an example, a role model to others I haven't reached yet with the message of this book; share the words of this book not only through your words, but also by your tangible examples of self-control. It is in that way that we, together, can not only shine our light but also spread it throughout the world.

CHAPTER 13

Sum it Up

We always begin with **The "Just Right" Checklist**:

1. **Breathing-Feelings Check-In**. Place one flat palm over your heart, and another flat palm over your belly. Pay attention to your breathing as it goes in and out. Is it even, or are you breathing too quickly/too slowly? Feel your heartbeat under your hand. Is it beating evenly, or is it racing? If your breathing and heartbeat is too fast, force yourself to take slow and even breaths. You can always try this strategy to check in and see how your body is responding to a feeling, or to try to even out your breathing and heart rate, when you are feeling **Slow and Tired**, **Fast and Emotional**, or **Fast and Wiggly**.

2. **Label your feeling/s.** Now that you have slowed down your breathing, you have allowed enough oxygen to enter your brain and given yourself time to think. How are you feeling? Think of the category first (**Fast and Emotional**, etc.). Picture where in your body your feeling is, and the color/s of this feeling. Then go more specifically (i.e. are you frustrated, sad, etc.). Label your feeling/s.

3. **Connect your feeling to your strategy.** Think of your feeling. Take the feeling in your hand, as if it were physical. Now, whatever strategy you choose, take the energy of that feeling and make it disappear through the use of the physical, tangible exercise or use of **tool**. This step directly relates to the idea of the **Mind-Body Connection**.

Feeling/s: _____

Strategy/ies: _____

We have four main categories of feelings: **Just Right**, **Slow and Tired**, **Fast and Emotional**, and **Fast and Wiggly**.

When we are feeling a strong physical or emotional feeling that is so intense that it is preventing us from completing what we want or need to do, that is when we are not **Just Right**.

When we are experiencing **Fast and Emotional** or **Fast and Wiggly** feelings, many times we are in *fight or flight*. To get out of *fight or flight*, we need to activate the *parasympathetic nervous system*. We do this through specific **Anywhere Body Breaks**, **tools**, and **Big Breaks (Yoga)**.

Tools are important, and they have their place in our daily lives. If you look around you, I think that you would see that many people already use them without realizing it. It is with the knowledge of what everyday objects are for, and how they can help us, that we can use them that more efficiently.

Your choice of times, activity types, and level of activity can depend on what part/s of the day are easiest and most difficult for you, how much time you have, as well as your physical activity capacity; try to schedule these exercises with those factors in mind.

Engaging in "big movement" activities before school (or at the start of your day in general) can help keep you feeling **Just Right** and happy. Participating in these activities after school (or at the end of the day, regardless) can help make homework, bedtime, and your overall evening easier and more stress-free.

Your light represents all of your hopes, positive feelings, and beautiful thoughts. It shines brightly when you feel happy, peaceful, content, attentive, and **Just Right**.

Sometimes, it takes some *dark times* (or difficult thoughts or feelings) to bring that light to the surface, and make it shine brightest. Use those moments as opportunities to be a positive influence on the world.

PART 2

FOR ADULTS

Acknowledgements

I find myself, yet again, thanking my stellar, patient, and brilliant commissioning editor, Rachel Menzies, whose endless understanding of the message of my books, patience in the process, endless editing hours, back-and-forth emails overseas, and true belief in the vision and hopeful impact of this work on the lives of others has helped to develop it from an idea spoken about through email and the occasional phone call to the actual book that you are reading at this very moment. Rachel—you are a rock star.

Thank you so much, yet again, to the amazing editorial staff, production, and marketing teams at Jessica Kingsley Publishers—I feel so blessed to work for a publishing company that values the benefit of publishing books that make a difference in the lives of others. I wake up so often in disbelief that I am afforded the opportunity to write books that can positively touch the lives of others.

To my family. As each day passes, I realize how important that connection truly is. I love you all.

To my grandfather 'Poppy', to the great-grandfather of my children, who has passed a little over a year since I am writing these words; I hope to honor you with this book. You were always my number one encourager to write. When I told you that I had no time—that I had three kids, a full-time job, no sleep as it is—you simply smiled your sweet smile and said, "And?" I truly believe that you are reading this in some way from Heaven. I hope that, three books later, I've done you proud.

To the love of my life, Joel—I've tried to put my thanks into words in previous books. As I type now, I am realizing that I can't. You do too much; you are too precious. There are no words to describe my love and appreciation for you.

Lastly, to Shayna, to Yosef, to Lianna. Writing, publishing, and impacting others through my words was my dream. I did it. It took a ton of hard work, and I put my heart and soul into my work. If I teach you anything by my example, I hope you can learn from this. I love you so, so, so much—and I believe in you.

For Parents and Caregivers—How to Get the Most Out of This Book

When asked what I do, my answer is usually: "Well, around five different jobs!" I'm a full-time pediatric occupational therapist, but I am also a full-time mom of three amazing kids (they are now eight, seven, and five). I am an author for Jessica Kingsley Publishers, and a blogger as well! I try my best to juggle it all, and it's all part of the journey, isn't it?

I truly believe that parents are children's best therapists. Nobody, I mean, *nobody*, knows or loves your child the way you do. Being a parent is the hardest, most amazing, exhausting, yet rewarding accomplishment that I can say that I've achieved. I commend you all. With all that in mind, I can merely suggest some ways for you to use this book; of course, you may find other ways that fit your lifestyle more fluidly! ☺

- I notice a significant difference in skill acquisition related to self-regulation among kids where strategies and exercises are consistently reinforced at home, in a multi-sensory manner, across different environments within their community. (I say this in the next section to the teachers, because it's true! Practice makes progress, so to speak.)

- There is a ton of content in this book. One good way to address the many different ideas would be to read/introduce one new self-regulatory strategy each week, for the duration of 42 weeks (one week per strategy/**tool**). This can be done either with your child, or they can read independently—depending on the child, and your lifestyle! At the beginning of the week, the strategy will be introduced, followed by a tangible reinforcements and visuals, where possible.

Over the course of the week, continue to reinforce the strategy in one or more of the following ways:

- Provide tangible visuals to accompany strategies, when applicable (i.e. a laminated visual from a chart in areas of the house that you mostly frequent—ours are in the kitchen and sensory nook, a bracelet with a laminated visual of a single strategy on string—hole-punched—you can have all members of your family wearing them, a **"Just Right" Self-Monitoring Checklist**, affirmation cards, etc.).

- Embed wording consistent with the strategy as appropriate.

- When starting off the day, remind your child/ren of the strategy or **tool** that they may use during a time that is predictably dysregulating for them or a potential trigger (i.e. recess, lunch, etc.): "Our strategy or tool of the week is _____. What is one way that we can use this today?"

- Ensure that all service providers, administrators, and cluster subject teachers, and anyone else servicing your child, are using the same language around self-regulation, and are using the same strategies and **tools**, when needed, to maximize the transfer of skills and self-regulation. Set up a meeting to discuss this—don't wait for their IEP meeting (if they have an IEP).

- Place the book, when not in use, in an area that is visually accessible to your kids—we have ours in our sensory nook in our den/cool down area.

- Kids model our actions, even more than our words. Model the use of the strategy through your own actions. For example, if you become angry, pause and model a strategy geared at that emotion. Afterwards, name it for your child. "I was feeling **Fast and Emotional** before, but I was able to calm down by using the _____ exercise."

For Teachers and Therapists—How to Get the Most Out of This Book

As an occupational therapist who has worked for a very long time in the school system, I can see a significant difference in skill acquisition related to self-regulation among students where strategies and exercises are consistently reinforced at the school level, in a multi-sensory manner, across the academic environment.

I understand the difficulty in being handed a book and being told: "Here! Make the magic happen!" So, here are some suggestions:

- Involve the class in learning one new self-regulatory strategy each week, for the duration of 42 weeks (one week per strategy/**tool**). At the beginning of the week, the strategy will be introduced, followed by a tangible reinforcements and visuals, where possible. Over the course of the week, continue to reinforce the strategy in one or more of the following ways:

  - Provide tangible visuals to accompany the strategies, when applicable (i.e. laminated visual from a chart at desks, a bracelet with a laminated visual of a single strategy on string—hole-punched—worn by all students, a **"Just Right" Self-Monitoring Checklist**, affirmation cards, etc.).

  - Display a visual of the strategy by a meeting area or the front of a classroom.

  - Embed wording consistent with the strategy, as appropriate, into academic talk.

  - Write a reminder on the board during the morning meeting (or include this as a class job!): "Our strategy or tool of the week is _____. What is one way that we can use this today?"

- Ensure that all service providers, administrators, and cluster subject teachers are using the same language around self-regulation, and are using the same strategies and **tools**, when needed, to maximize the transfer of skills and self-regulation.

- Place the book, when not in use, in an area that is visually accessible to all children. Have different students read it aloud to the class. Consider making each chapter into a class discussion, building on community, and reinforcing the idea that everyone has their "stuff" and can benefit from a little help.

- Involve families in understanding learned strategies and **tools** so that there is consistency between what you are doing in class and the language that is being used at home.

- Before beginning the unit, explain the purpose behind what you are teaching the children, and how these strategies can help them in their daily lives. Stress the importance of the home-school connection, and explain that you will send home visuals of strategies taught (and examples of places to put them around the home), and information on what you teach each week.

- Share the visual of the strategy being worked on, preferably enlarged, with the families of the children in your class.

- An interesting way to share a little about what you are working on would be through a weekly newsletter in which you can explain the name of the strategy, highlighted that week and ways children are using it in the classroom. The newsletter may also contain suggestions from this book that help reinforce self-regulation, sensory processing, social-emotional learning and overall independence, emotional health, independence in activities of daily living, and social-emotional growth.

  - Consider purchasing this book in order to have all the strategies, **tools**, and visuals available, whenever you need it.

  - Ensure that you are reinforcing the strategy of the week throughout your daily interactions with your child. For example, when you start the day, try to anticipate together a time during the day that the strategy may come in handy.

  - Model the use of the strategy through your own actions. For example, if you become angry, pause and model a strategy geared at that emotion. Afterwards, name it for your child. "I was feeling **Fast and Emotional** before, but I was able to calm down by using the _____ exercise."

Maslow's Hierarchy of Human Needs, and its Connection to Child Development

Abraham Maslow was an American psychologist who created Maslow's Hierarchy of Human Needs. This theory works on a priority model of practice—that is, you cannot address a level higher in the pyramid before the lower levels have been taken care of.

Maslow's Hierarchy of Human Needs[1]

Now, how does this apply to the children we live with or work with? It is important to note that, like us, children have many physiological and emotional needs. There is often an inconsistency with regards to how often and how effectively these needs are met, depending on both internal and external factors.

---

1   See www.saybrook.edu/?s=maslow

As educators, therapists, and parents/caregivers, it is important that we ensure that we are doing our best to meet the most basic levels of the pyramid for these children before expecting them to achieve the higher levels, which includes esteem and self-actualization (which has major academic implications). Some lower level items to consider are as follows.

Basic needs questions to consider

1. Are the children coming in getting enough sleep?

2. Are the children drinking enough water throughout the day?

3. Are the children eating a nutritious breakfast? Are they eating healthy snacks and meals? (Including food with omega 3 fatty acids.)

4. Is it an optimal temperature in the classroom/home setting?

5. Do the children feel secure and/or safe and secure throughout the school day?

Some suggestions to address these concerns
Sleep

- Consider coming up with a sleep schedule if sleep is a concern, and if you find that a few of your students/clients (or your own children) appear to be sleepy on a consistent basis.

- *Blue light spectrum and sleep.* According to an article published by Harvard Health Publications, "Blue light has a dark side." Blue light suppresses melatonin most powerfully out of all lights on the spectrum. The Harvard researchers and their colleagues conducted an experiment that compared the effects of 6.5 hours of exposure to blue light versus exposure to green light. The blue light suppressed melatonin for twice as long as the green light; it also shifted circadian rhythms by twice as much (3 hours versus 1.5 hours). Some modifications for nighttime routines could therefore be the following: avoid looking at bright screens 2–3 hours before bed (this includes iPads, computers, and television); use a red-light nightlight (if the child uses a nightlight); and ensure that the child has significant exposure to bright light during the day.[2]

---

2   See www.mayoclinic.org/healthy-lifestyle/childrens-health/in-depth/nutrition-for-kids/art-20049335

Drinking water

Ensure that children are drinking water throughout the day, both inside and outside the classroom. A way to do this is to allow them to bring in water bottles, and to use them during classroom time. Water bottles with a resistant straw will help with attention, and prevent spilling.

Nutritious food

Here are some suggestions for healthy and "brain food":

Healthy food

- apricots
- avocados
- raspberries
- tomatoes
- cantaloupe melon
- cranberry juice
- raisins
- figs
- lemons and limes
- onions
- artichokes
- ginger
- broccoli
- spinach
- bok choy
- pumpkin or squash
- garlic
- arugula
- wheat germ/oatmeal
- quinoa
- nuts and peanuts
- lentils
- yogurt and skim milk
- salmon and shrimps[3]

Brain food

- Oatmeal. This cereal has high fiber and protein content, and has been associated with improved special and short-term memory tests, as well as auditory attention tests.

---

3   See   www.health.harvard.edu/newsletters/Harvard_Health_Letter/2012/May/blue-light-has-a-dark-side

- Blueberries (if they don't like them fresh, try them frozen!) contain antioxidants associated with increased memory and cognitive functioning.

- Eggs are high in protein and choline (which is important for memory stem cells).

- Flaxseeds are a great source of omega 3 fatty acids (associated with improved learning capacity). You could try sprinkling them on cereal.[5]

Temperature

Be mindful that if you are cold, the children in your classroom and/or house will feel that even more. Do your best to regulate the temperature as best as you can, and moderate your expectations with regards to their attention and overall self-regulation.

Safety and security

Providing children with certain rituals and routines that are consistent and predictable is a relatively simple way to help increase feelings of safety and security.

---

4   See www.greatschools.org/parenting/health-nutrition/1584-four-brain-foods-kids-love.gs

Simple Supports to Promote Overall Self-Regulation

There are so many ways to implement universal design for learning, environmental adaptations, and/or simple modifications to everyday routines at home, in the classroom, or the therapy space that can make significant therapeutic gains for your child/student.

The following suggestions and supports offer options to further nurture skills discussed and developed through the strategies and **tools** outlined earlier, in Part 1, in a manner that can be often provided to all members of your family/classroom/therapeutic community (in the least restrictive manner). I hope that you will find that they are easily embedded into your already-busy schedule, resulting in greater consistently, flow, and follow-through.

- *Use natural or incandescent lighting.* An incandescent light bulb is an electric light that emits a warm glow that is notably less harsh than fluorescent light bulbs (with a fuller spectrum of light). Fluorescent lights emit a poorer quality of light (with a limited spectrum). Lack of exposure to a broad spectrum of lights can affect our bodily functions, such as our circadian rhythm (think sleep!). If that is not an option, try to open blinds and turn off one of the fluorescent lights.

- *Use of low-frequency music to promote self-regulation and a sense of calm.* Binaural music (where it crosses from one ear to another) with headphones works to improve focus.

- *Provide a variety of soft pillows, mats, and cushions* of varying sizes, shapes, and textures for children to access during reading, writing, interactive play, etc.

- *Ensure that you are not having students or your own children sit longer than they are developmentally able to.* A good strategy for this is to use a visual timer set approximately one minute per year of age (i.e. if the group of children are aged eight, I will set the timer for eight minutes). After eight minutes, allow them to get up and engage in a controlled movement-based activity that incorporates **proprioceptive**, **crossing midline** and **vestibular inputs** (see Chapter 11, pp.87–99, for more information).

- *"Mirror-me" movements.* Tell the children that they should copy your movements so exactly that it is as if they are your mirror. This process not only forces them to slow down and work on body control, but activates mirror neurons in the brain, which is important for overall improved attention.

- *Mandalas.* As a relaxation or meditation exercise, provide your child/ren with mandalas that are appropriate to their level of fine motor skills, and allow them to simply color for a specified amount of time. Tell them that it isn't a rush—that they have time over several days to finish, that the point is to stay in the lines, and to take the time to focus on themselves and take a break from the day. You can combine this activity with playing low-frequency music.

- *Children spend too much time sitting upright.* Consider allowing them to attend to instruction, complete schoolwork, homework, and play laying prone (belly on the floor), standing, or in alternate positions.

- *Consider using the* **Big Breaks/Yoga** *poses listed in this book as part of a consistent routine.* You can try implementing this in the morning before school, as part of a morning classroom schedule, as an after lunch/recess cool-down classroom activity, to break up the long hours of homework, or as a before-bedtime ritual. This will work to not only improve overall physical and emotional regulation, but provide that consistency and feeling of safety that comes with predictable routines.

- *Proud Board.* Have a "Proud Board" in your home, therapy space, or classroom. Place students' names, with space to showcase their favorite work that they are most proud of. (Note: if you make it magnetic, they can easily put on and take off their "proud pieces".)

This is a picture of our family Proud Board. ☺

- *Our classroom community/family motivators book!* As a whole-class or family activity, talk about feeling confident. You can use concrete examples from day-to-day classroom/family experiences, or use motivational quotes that you have researched online. As a next step, your class can create an "Our classroom community/family motivators book!" Have each child/group of children write a motivational or inspirational quote or saying. They can illustrate it, or you can take a photo of them representing that quote. For example, if the quote is talking about perseverance, photograph a child or a few children working hard in an area that feels challenging for them. In times of decreased confidence or emotional dysregulation, you could redirect them to take a look at this book as a confidence-booster!

- *Provide access to quiet areas in the classroom and home setting (pair it with a visual timer).* This can be as simple as a private work area (noise-reducing headphones paired with a correl (visual-stimuli blocker)), or an individual quiet space desk away from other students. This could be a tent—a table covered with a blanket or blocked with pillows.

- *Create a cool-down/sensory area within the classroom and home setting.* Observe signs of decreased physical or emotional regulation, and when signs of this begin to emerge, direct the child to this area. Items you may want to include could be bean bags (to provide a bean bag squish), putty, a lava lamp/aquarium light, drawing pad/crayons, lavender/vanilla-scented materials (calming scents), weighted lap pad/blanket, glitter jar, box of kinetic sand, etc.). This area can also be a place for your child to work independently on schoolwork, and when they are feeling emotionally dysregulated.

- Consider creating an *emotional-control toolbox* with different items (e.g. putty/Play-Doh, a small note pad and a few crayons, mini-glitter jar, small stress ball, etc.), for your child/ren to take to certain environments that you know may prove to be triggers. Provide it to them when you notice the first signs of dysregulation, and coach them into using them, with fading prompts.

- *Positive affirmations jar.* We have a home- and therapy-based jar of positive affirmations. There are stones and cards with different positive affirmations, and they are able to be easily accessed, as they are in places that are easily frequented, such as our kitchen, cool-down areas, etc.

All charts in the following appendix section with a symbol are available to be downloaded from www.jkp.com. You can photocopy these and laminate them to bring along with you wherever you go, especially if you are traveling somewhere that you anticipate your child may have difficulty.

"Just Right" Checklist

This can be especially beneficial if laminated for durability/portability, and put onto a keyring with other printables, if desired, to carry around across different settings. You can download the checklist and place it around different settings, to improve the transfer of the steps of this skill of self-regulation—simply laminate or place in a plastic sheet protector!

"Just-Right" Checklist

1) **Breathing-Feelings Check-In.** Place one flat palm over your heart, and another flat palm over your belly. Pay attention to your breathing as it goes in and out. Is it even, or are you breathing too quickly/too slowly? Feel your heartbeat under your hand. Is it beating evenly, or is it racing? If your breathing and heart beat is too fast, force yourself to take slow and even breaths (read the instructions for "forced exhalation breathing" on p.35). You can always try this strategy to check in and see how your body is responding to a feeling, or to try to even out your breathing and heart rate, when you are feeling **Slow and Tired**, **Fast and Emotional**, or **Fast and Wiggly**.

2) **Label your feeling/s.** Now that you have slowed down your breathing, you have allowed enough oxygen to enter your brain and given yourself time to think. How are you feeling? Think of the category first (**Fast and Emotional**, etc.). Picture where in your body your feeling is, and the color/s of this feeling. Then go more specifically (i.e. are you frustrated, sad, etc.). Label your feeling/s.

3) **Connect your feeling to your strategy.** Think of your feeling. Take the feeling in your hand, as if it were physical. Now, whatever strategy you choose (and we will go into detail in the following chapters), take the energy of that feeling and make it disappear through the use of the physical, tangible exercise or use of **tool**. This step directly relates to the idea of the **Mind-Body Connection.**

Feeling/s: _____

Strategy/ies: _____

"My List of Ten" Card

This can be especially beneficial if laminated for durability/portability, and put onto a keyring with other printables, if desired, to carry around across different settings. You can download it and place it around different settings, including the classroom, therapy room (and even the fridge) for the child/ren to write down positive attributes about themselves—simply laminate or put in a plastic sheet protector!

My List of Ten

1) _____

2) _____

3) _____

4) _____

5) _____

6) _____

7) _____

8) _____

9) _____

10) _____

Positive Affirmations

This can be especially beneficial if laminated for durability/portability, and put onto a keyring with other printables, if desired, to carry around across different setting, or to use as a bookmark. You can download them and place them around different settings, including the classroom, therapy room (and even the fridge) for the child/ren to repeat the affirmations about themselves or write their own—simply laminate or put in a plastic sheet protector!

Affirmations ☺

"The glass is half full."

"I can't change other people—just myself."

"I make my part of the world a better place just by being in it."

"I am confident."

"I know myself as a person and as a learner."

"I can do anything I put my mind to."

"I have self-control."

"I love myself for who I am."

"I am focused."

"I am a valuable member of my community."

_____

_____

"Just Right"
Self-Monitoring Checklist

This can be especially beneficial if laminated for durability/portability, and put onto a keyring with other printables, if desired, to carry around across different settings. You can download it and place it around different settings, to improve transfer of the steps of this skill of self-monitoring around the process of self-regulation—simply laminate.

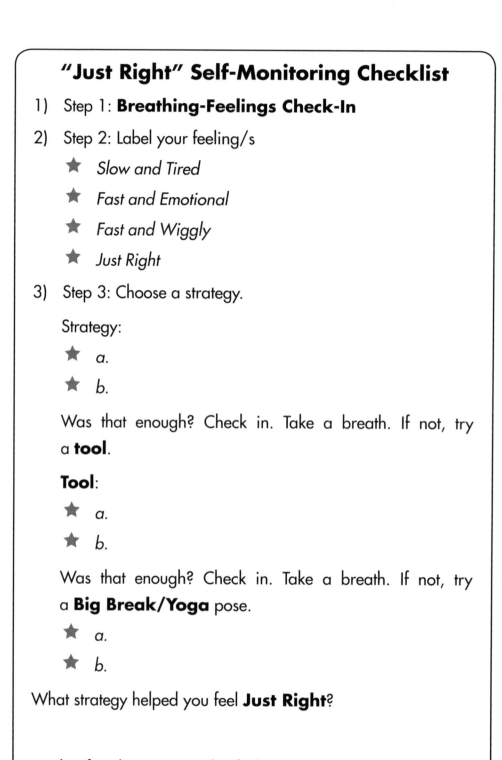

"Just Right" Self-Monitoring Checklist

1) Step 1: **Breathing-Feelings Check-In**

2) Step 2: Label your feeling/s

   ★ *Slow and Tired*

   ★ *Fast and Emotional*

   ★ *Fast and Wiggly*

   ★ *Just Right*

3) Step 3: Choose a strategy.

   Strategy:

   ★ a.

   ★ b.

   Was that enough? Check in. Take a breath. If not, try a **tool**.

   Tool:

   ★ a.

   ★ b.

   Was that enough? Check in. Take a breath. If not, try a **Big Break/Yoga** pose.

   ★ a.

   ★ b.

What strategy helped you feel **Just Right**?

Try that first the next time this feeling comes up! ☺

At a Glance Desk Strip Reminders—Anywhere Body Breaks, Tools, and Big Breaks/Yoga

These are great to place either on desks and/or throughout a variety of environments to increase the transfer of skills. You may want to color-code these strips, to make it easier to visualize. For example, you may want to download and print the **Slow and Tired** strip on *blue* paper, the **Fast and Emotional** on *red* or *pink* paper, and the **Fast and Wiggly** on *green* paper. Consider laminating for increased durability.

Slow and Tired (with visuals)

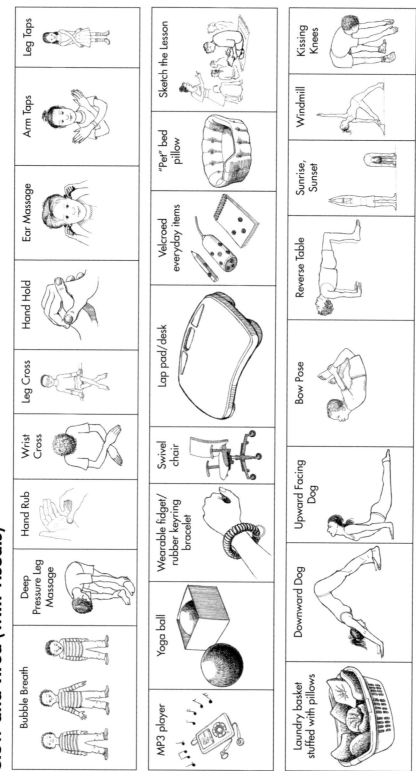

| Bubble Breath | Deep Pressure Leg Massage | Hand Rub | Wrist Cross | Leg Cross | Hand Hold | Ear Massage | Arm Taps | Leg Taps |

| MP3 player | Yoga ball | Wearable fidget/ rubber keyring bracelet | Swivel chair | Lap pad/desk | Velcroed everyday items | "Pet" bed pillow | Sketch the Lesson |

| Laundry basket stuffed with pillows | Downward Dog | Upward Facing Dog | Bow Pose | Reverse Table | Sunrise, Sunset | Windmill | Kissing Knees |

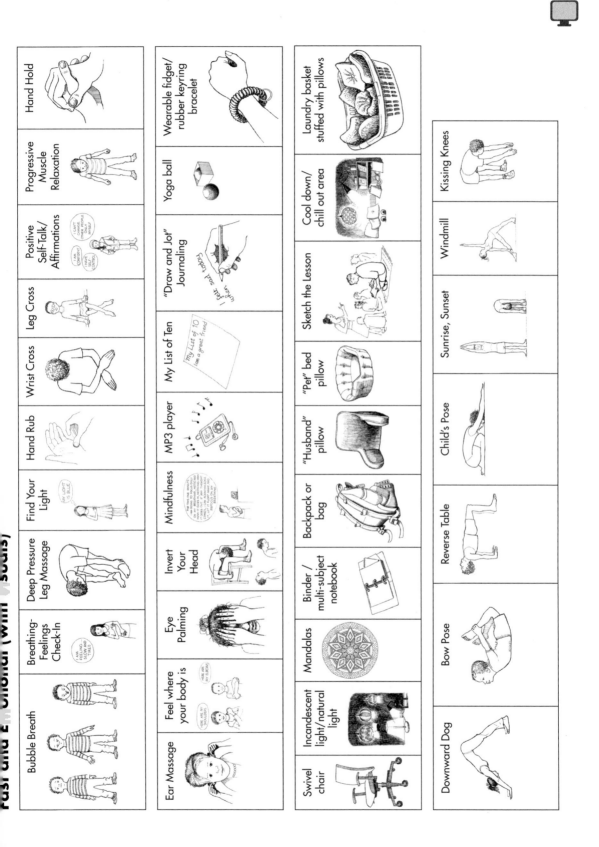

Bubble Breath	Breathing-Feelings Check-In	Deep Pressure Leg Massage	Find Your Light	Hand Rub	Wrist Cross	Leg Cross	Positive Self-Talk/ Affirmations	Progressive Muscle Relaxation	Hand Hold

Ear Massage	Feel where your body is	Eye Palming	Invert Your Head	Mindfulness	Mandalas	MP3 player	My List of Ten	"Draw and Jot" Journaling	Yoga ball	Wearable fidget/ rubber keyring bracelet

Swivel chair	Incandescent light/natural light	Binder / multi-subject notebook	Backpack or bag	"Husband" pillow	"Pet" bed pillow	Sketch the Lesson	Cool down/ chill out area	Laundry basket stuffed with pillows

Downward Dog	Bow Pose	Reverse Table	Child's Pose	Sunrise, Sunset	Windmill	Kissing Knees

Fast and Wiggly (with visuals)

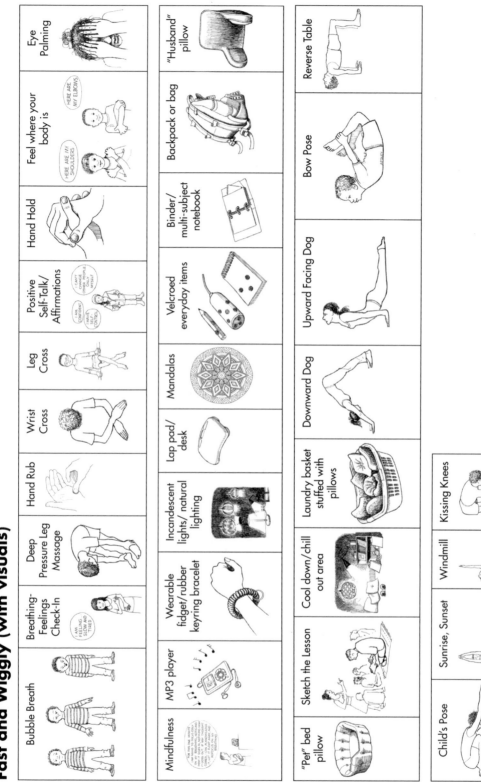

At a Glance Bracelet Reminders (for Anywhere Body Breaks Only)

These are great for the user to wear consistently across a variety of environments to increase the transfer of skills. You may want to color-code these bracelet strips, to make it easier to visualize. For example, you may want to download and print the **Slow and Tired** strip on *blue* paper, the **Fast and Emotional** on *red* or *pink* paper, and the **Fast and Wiggly** on *green* paper. Consider laminating for increased durability.

Slow and Tired (with visuals)

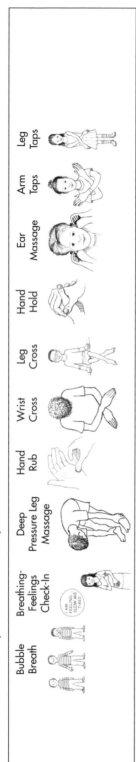

Fast and Emotional (with visuals)

At a Glance Bracelet Reminders (for Anywhere Body Breaks Only)

These are great for the user to wear consistently across a variety of environments to increase the transfer of skills. You may want to color-code these bracelet strips, to make it easier to visualize. For example, you may want to download and print the **Slow and Tired** strip on *blue* paper, the **Fast and Emotional** on *red* or *pink* paper, and the **Fast and Wiggly** on *green* paper. Consider laminating for increased durability.

Slow and Tired (with visuals)

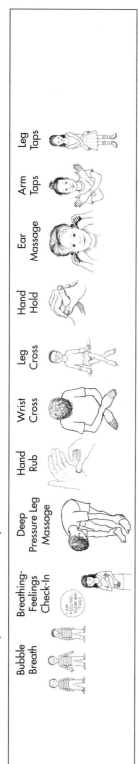

Fast and Emotional (with visuals)

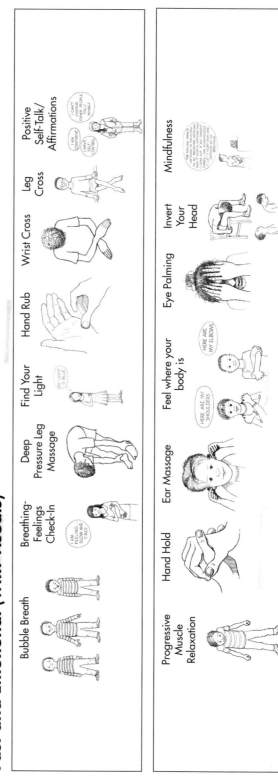

Fast and Wiggly (with visuals)

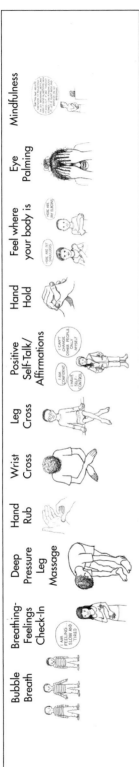

| Bubble Breath | Breathing-Feelings Check-In | Deep Pressure Leg Massage | Hand Rub | Wrist Cross | Leg Cross | Positive Self-Talk/ Affirmations | Hand Hold | Feel where your body is | Eye Palming | Mindfulness |

"Draw and Jot" Journaling Card

This is a great **tool** to vent your feelings and to let them out, so to speak. You can write them out, jot out a few words, or draw a representation. If you are using the cards, laminate 1–3 and attach them to your keyring. If you use a thin-tip dry erase marker that you can place in your pocket, this can be a portable "journal-on-the-go."

If you are using the sheet templates (that you can download), on the top of the sheets, they have an option of going through the following process:

1. **"Breathing-Feelings Check-In"**

2. Label your feeling

3. Connect your feeling/s to your strategy

4. Write/jot/draw it out!

"Draw and Jot" Journaling

Step 1: **Breathing-Feelings Check-In**

Step 2: Label your feeling/s

⭐ *Slow and Tired*   ⭐ *Fast and Wiggly*

⭐ *Fast and Emotional*   ⭐ *Just Right*

Step 3: Connect your feeling to your strategy.

Step 4: Think for a moment—what strategies can I use today to keep myself feeling **Just Right** and in control?

_____

_____

_____

_____

_____

_____

_____

_____

_____

_____

_____

_____

_____

_____

_____

Lauren Brukner is a Senior Occupational Therapist who lives in New York City with her husband and her three children.

Lauren has appeared as a guest on The Autism Show, The Manhattan Neighborhood Network's School-Home Connection, and the Matt Townsend Show on Sirius XM Radio.

Her award-winning books have been listed as resources on websites such as *Real Simple Magazine, Inc. Magazine, Marie Claire, Everyday Health, AOL's Health and Wellness, MSN Health, Mothering.com, About.com,* and *Friendship Circle,* as well as numerous school district curricula around the world.

Lauren specializes in sensory integration and self-regulation strategies for children and young people, and their implementation in home, school, and community settings. She holds advanced training and certification in Integrated Listening Systems, and is a Certified Screener for Irlen Syndrome/Scotopic Sensitivity.

Lauren is the author of *The Kids' Guide to Staying Awesome and In Control* and *How to Be a Superhero Called Self-Control,* which won the gold seal in the Mom's Choice Awards, 2016 for family friendly media, products, and services.

Lauren is a contributing writer to *The Huffington Post* and *Autism Parenting Magazine* and blogs at www.awesomeandincontrol.com.

When she is not writing or "therapizing," Lauren can often be found going on a weekend adventure with her family, having a good dance party with her kids, or curled up with an engrossing book and a great cup of coffee. It all depends on the day.